THE ANSWER

Jesus has a plan for each of us. His voice rings out to us, and we have but to commit ourselves wholly to Him to hear the answers and to feel His love and protection in every corner of our lives.

THE ANSWER

Stuart Dearsley

ARTHUR H. STOCKWELL LTD.
Elms Court   Ilfracombe   Devon
Established 1898

British Library Cataloguing-in-Publication Data.
A catalogue record for this book is available
from the British Library.

To,

All my family and friends for inspiring me and encouraging me in my writing, and above all else, to God for giving me the gift to be able to write songs and poetry for other's enjoyment.

ISBN 0 7223 3062-6

Printed in Great Britain by
Arthur H. Stockwell Ltd.
Elms Court   Ilfracombe
Devon

CONTENTS

I CAN'T DO IT

I can't do it.
Yes you can.
No, I really can't do it.
Yes you can,

Just give it all to him,
And he will help you out;
No use holding on to it,
Cause he knows what you're about.

If you let something get hold of you,
It will hurt you in the end;
If you let Lord Jesus help you,
Then you'll be on the mend.

Nothing is too hard for him,
That's what the Bible says;
Put all of your trust in him,
And he will show he cares.

You may think it's quite difficult,
But he's not that far away;
He's right there in your situation,
And hears every word you say.

FROM THIS DAY ON

Not long ago,
I looked at my life,
A life full of trouble,
A life full of strife;
I realised then,
I should change my ways,
I realised then,
What I had to say,

From this day on,
I know he's there,
From this day on,
I know he cares;
From this day on,
I'll praise his name,
From this day on,
He'll take the blame.

He didn't have to,
But he did it for me,
He gave his life,
So that I could see;
One way forward,
That I could go,
One way forward,
So that I would know,

From this day on,
I know he's there,
From this day on,
I know he cares;
From this day on,
I'll praise his name,
From this day on,
He'll take the blame.

We sometimes think,
That we know best,
That we know better,
Than all the rest;
Cause one thing now,
That I have learnt,
The grace of God,
Just can't be earnt.

If we listen carefully,
When we hear his cry,
He'll help us out,
And he'll tell us why;
Don't look to this world,
Just follow me,
Don't look to this world,
And you will see, cause,

From this day on,
I know he's there,
From this day on,
I know he cares;
From this day on,
I'll praise his name,
From this day on,
He'll take the blame.

CROSS TO BEAR

He stood before the governor,
And the elders were there too.
'Is it true,' Pilate said to Jesus,
'That you're the King of the Jews?'

Jesus did not answer,
So Pilate said again,
'Don't you hear what the men are saying?
Are you not going to answer them?'

Jesus stood in silence,
And Pilate turned to the crowd,
'Who do you want released to you?'
'Barabbas' they shouted out loud.

Pilate looked at Jesus,
And he knew he wouldn't win.
'What shall I do with Jesus then?'
The crowd shouted 'Crucify him.'

Then Pilate took some water,
And then he washed his hands,
He handed Jesus over to them,
'I take no responsibility for this man.'

The soldiers they took Jesus,
To prepare him for his death;
They made him a crown of thorns,
And placed it on his head.

Then Jesus started on the road,
To the place they call the skull;
The cross upon his shoulders,
A cross too heavy to hold.

He had a cross to bear,
But he didn't really care,
About the pain he went through,
Cause he did it for you,
The one he loves so much.

Jesus hung there on the cross,
And the people gathered round;
Some stood hurling insults,
While others cried on the ground.

The hours slowly passed by,
And then the ninth hour came;
Darkness filled the earth,
And Jesus cried out again,

'Eloi, Eloi, Lama Sabachthani,'
The people they couldn't believe,
As Jesus spoke out loud, 'My God. My God.
Why have you forsaken me?'

The earth it began to shake,
As Jesus breathed his last,
The crowd looked on in horror,
While others walked on past.

Then Jesus was taken down from the cross,
And taken to Joseph's tomb,
A tomb he'd recently built,
And one with a lot of room.

Three more days they passed by,
And then the miracle came,
Jesus Christ he conquered death,
And was risen to life again.

Jesus went to Galilee,
And the people followed him too,
'Do not be afraid,' he said,
'I did it all for you.'

GIVE YOUR LIFE

You're walking down the street,
Just as cool as you like,
When someone walks over,
And shouts out 'Hi!'
They say they're a Christian,
And you turn away,
Just turn back round,
It's your lucky day.

They say they know someone,
Who died for you.
You laugh in their face,
And shout out who?
Jesus was his name,
And he died on a cross;
You push them out the way,
And walk right off.

Deep down low,
You want them to follow,
Cause deep inside,
Your heart feels hollow;
What are you missing?
You don't quite know.
You think to yourself,
I'll give it a go.
You turn back round,
And walk their way.
Your voice speaks out,
What did you say?
There's more to life,
Than drink and sex.
You say alright,
Then what comes next?

Give your Life
To Jesus the Lord;
Take this step
You'll never be bored.
Your life will change,
You'll never be the same,
As when that day
That Jesus Christ came.

You go to Church,
It's better than you think;
You can't believe your eyes,
And you have to blink;
A sight you've seen,
Like never before;
You think to yourself,
I'll come back for more.

Many years later, you're
Still right there,
Praising the Lord God,
Without a care.
One day you'll be,
Out on that street,
And you'll spot a person,
That you'd like to meet.

You'll walk right over,
And shout out 'Hi!'
I'd like to tell you,
How Jesus changed my life.
It's changed for the better,
Cause now that I know,
That the Lord Jesus Christ,
Is the only way to go.

NO OTHER WAY

Fact or Fiction?
Just an addiction.
Way to go?
Don't you know.
You gotta make a choice,
Can't just roll,
Decide which way,
Or end up in a hole,

At the end of the day,
You gotta choose;
One way stops,
One way moves.
You can't choose both,
You gotta take one;
So make the right choice,
And choose the son.

There is no other way,
To be free from all sin;
Choose the son of God,
And you can only win.
So take the first prize,
And then you'll really know,
Peace in your heart,
Is the only way to go.

Full of pride,
You don't need that;
Change your ways,
Or fall down flat.
Get it right,
And stand out tall;
Get it wrong,
And you will fall.

Make your choice,
And make it right;
Go the right way,
And you'll see the light.
One way only,
That you can go;
Live your life,
In the best way known.

CAN'T GET ENOUGH

I wanna tell you something,
And it's gotta be today,
If you stand near or around me,
Then you'll hear me say,
I don't like swearing,
And I don't take drugs,
That's a stupid game to play,
And only one for mugs.
I don't mind a drink,
But I don't drink a lot,
Cause drink too much,
And it'll put you in a spot.
If you drink one too many,
Then you don't know what you do,
You make yourself look stupid,
And everyone looks at you.
Stop before you reach the line,
And then you'll have no worries;
Take one step over the line,
You'll be the one who's sorry.

Can't get enough,
Of the Christian way;
I live my life for Jesus,
Every minute of the day.
I'll show you all my friends,
And they will tell you too,
Live your life for Jesus,
It's the best thing you can do.

You may think it's well hard,
To be seen to smoke;
It'll cost you a packet,
And you'll end up broke.
Take one puff,
And you'll find it hard to stop;
Smoke far too many,
And you'll be the one to drop.
There's far much more to life,
Than this whole world can give;
Check out your ways,
And how you wish to live.
Other people suffer,
By the things you choose to do;
Smoking can effect,
More people than just you.
Drinking can cause death,
Drugs can do that too;
So give all of it up,
Before it gets hold of you.

THE BEST IS YET TO COME

The nights are getting darker,
The world is getting worse.
Nations fight each other,
Are we living under a curse?

America thinks it knows best;
The Russians do as well.
All the others follow;
It's like a living hell.

People starve in Africa;
As countries fall apart,
Civil wars break out,
And this is only the start.

The major powers send their money.
Is this the only way,
To help a world that's dying,
A world that's falling away?

The best is yet to come,
And it's not too far away;
The return of the living son,
So let's all shout and say,

The best is yet to come,
The final chapter's near;
No matter what the world may say,
The Bible makes it clear.

Many spread the word of hope,
And in what they believe;
Religion destroying a world,
That now can only grieve.

Who would have thought,
All those years ago,
That a planet full of beauty,
Would end up on death row?

There's no hope for it now,
All we can do is see,
A world that's falling apart,
A world no longer free.

So in these final days,
Let's do our best for him;
Spread the word of the living God,
And turn this world from sin.

EYES AWAY

Turn on the television,
It's not what you want to see,
9.30 in the evening,
And sex and violence rains free;
You reach out for the controls,
To change to the other side,
Part of you says leave it on,
But another voice says inside,

Eyes away,
You really don't want to see,
What's in your line of sight;
Resist temptation and it shall flee,
Don't give in to the lies of the night.

You go to the cinema,
With all of your mates,
Appearing on the big screen,
Is a film they say is great;
As the film goes on by,
You wish that you weren't there,
Your mind says look it's great,
Your heart says get out of there.

Eyes away,
You really don't want to see,
What's in your line of sight;
Resist temptation and it shall flee,
Don't give in to the lies of the night.

Picking up the Sunday papers,
You open up the very first page;
Full of things you don't wanna see,
You feel like you're trapped in a cage.
Everywhere you turn your eyes,
Are things you want to quit;
You know what you've got to do,
Just walk away from it.

IN HIS IMAGE

When you look around, what do you see?
People of different colours;
Black and White, Yellow and Brown,
But does it really matter?

Everybody is different,
But we're all the same inside;
No matter where you go,
There is no need to hide.

You might be tall, you might be small,
What difference does it make?
Cause one thing's sure, no matter what you think,
You are not a fake.

He made you like you are,
You're beautiful in his sight.
Why argue with the creator?
You know he's always right.

If we were all fat, if we were all thin,
What fun would it be.
He made you how he wanted you,
So just take a look and see.

He loves you like you are.
Why would you want to change?
He made you in his sight,
So don't rearrange your life.

He made you in his image.
How could he not succeed?
He made you in his image.
What else do you need?

BEST FRIEND

Whenever I have a problem,
I know that you are there;
Whenever my heart is troubled,
I know that you really care.
Every single minute of the day,
I can turn to you,
Knowing that you are there for me,
And knowing that your love is true.

You are there in my sorrow,
You never leave me on my own;
Even when I'm happy,
Your glorious love is shown.
What more could I want,
To make my life complete?
A friend as good as you,
No one could surely meet.

Cause you are my best friend,
And I know you won't let me down;
Cause you are my best friend,
The best there is in any town.

DIAMOND IN THE ROUGH

We may think we're all alone,
When there's trouble all around;
When we stand up in situations,
And we wished we stayed underground.
God will always be there for us,
And we must remember that,
He won't leave us stranded there,
We will never be trapped.
It's like being a diamond in the rough,
We're different from all the rest;
Cause a diamond in the rough,
Really is the best.
If we really stick with God,
He will never let us down;
Be a light in the darkness,
Even if you feel like a clown.
Stand out from everybody else,
Be different from everyone;
Don't worry what people may say,
If you stand up for the son.

A BETTER PLACE

Sorrow and grief, anguish and pain,
We all get that same feeling again;
When someone we know is called back home,
A time when often we all feel alone.

We all have to go at sometime,
But we'll never know when it is;
Our number will be up some day,
There's nothing we can do or say.

Today, tomorrow or even next week,
This year or the next.
Who knows when the call will come?
It's written nowhere in the text.

The Bible won't tell us when it is,
But it will make us prepared;
Friends and relatives may have gone,
But it's really like going to bed.

One day we will wake up,
And we'll be in a different place;
No more tears and sadness,
Everybody with smiles on their face.

When all of it happens,
We will never know;
But if you believe the word of God,
It's a place where you can go.

We're going to a better place,
Better than here on earth;
We'll be going to join them there,
Cause it happens to us all.

MAKE A DIFFERENCE

I look out of my window,
And what can I see?
I see the world around,
And it's looking at me.
I only wish that I could,
Do it some good;
I think to myself,
And realise I could,
Make a Difference.

It may be hard at first,
But don't put it off;
If we don't do it now,
It could all soon be lost.
We gotta go along,
With what we know is right;
Make a stand for Jesus,
And put this world back right,
Make a Difference.

NAZARETH HILL

On Nazareth Hill,
The lights they still shine out;
On Nazareth Hill,
The people still come to see what it's all about.

Darkness falls and the rain beats down,
On the place where it all began,
2,000 years further on, and
Still the place is around.

Where Mary and Joseph first laid eyes,
On each other that fateful night;
Little did they know what was going on,
History in the making and a wonderful sight.

Nothing much has changed since then,
The lost can still be found;
Preaching the gospel's still the same,
Even though we're on Holy ground.

But Mary and Joseph had to go,
Where the Lord God, he told them so;
And off they went to Bethlehem,
But still they remember the place called home.

WAITING FOR A DAY

It all seems so easy,
In the desires of our heart,
As we sit around and wait,
For the day when it all will start.
Do we wanna step out,
And make the first move?
Is it the right decision,
What we really wanna do?

Living our lives around our dreams,
Watching the world pass us by,
Not knowing for certain,
Whether to laugh or cry.
Our lives change around us,
Are we thinking straight?
Our feelings are taking over,
Don't wanna make a mistake.

Time stops for no-one,
We gotta face the facts;
The odds are up against us,
We might be on the right track,
Setting our sights,
On a distant dream;
Knowing full well,
That it's not how it seems.

Waiting for a day,
That will never come;
A longing hope within our minds,
That this must be the one.
Sometimes it's not meant to be,
We're looking in the wrong place;
We gotta change our ideas,
Cause there is another way.

GET OFF THAT ROUTINE

We get up in the morning,
To live our daily lives,
Doing the same as yesterday,
And not really knowing why.
Every day's gotta be different,
To the day before;
As we live our lives for God,
We know there's so much more.

Get off that routine,
Live a different life,
Forget about yesterday,
Although it may have been nice.
Routines don't change you,
Only you can do that;
A bit of variation,
And you won't look back.

Today is just another day,
And there's so much more,
That today can offer,
Than any day before;
Do something different,
And you may be surprised;
Do something different and
It could change your life.

A BACK-SEAT DRIVER

A back-seat driver,
We don't wanna be;
A front-seat driver,
Is what God wants for me.
We can sit in the back,
And say which way to go.
But which way are we going,
Do we really know?

Where are we going?
Where have we been?
We gotta take a lead in things,
And not just be seen;
To be going along with the crowd,
We may be really loud,
But when it comes down to it,
Are we in the front seat?

We may be seen
With our hands in the air,
Waving them like,
We just don't care;
But it's down in your heart,
Where it really counts.
Are you leading your life,
Or just acting the clown?

We must be the driver,
In all that we do;
We must look forward,
To who looks at you.
You be the one,
Who is at the controls;
There's no other way forward,
You can't just roll.

BLAMELESS

Many people try so hard for his love,
To always be seen to be doing good;
But the one thing that they are forgetting,
Is that this is the wrong way.
For you can't get to Heaven by doing good,
Otherwise many people most certainly would;
All you have to do is say a prayer,
And then you'll almost certainly be there.

Cause it's by his grace that we are saved,
And not by the works that we do;
Let's lift our eyes to him,
And let's go the right way.
There's only one way to get to God,
To many people that might seem odd;
But say you're sorry and if you really do,
Then he'll make quite sure there's a place for you.

You're blameless in his sight,
No longer have to fight,
Cause what he's given you,
Is yours to keep.
It's nothing you can achieve,
By the works that you do;
If you stand and confess before him,
You're blameless in his sight.

IS THIS HOW IT SHOULD BE?

When their back is turned,
What do you say?
When they're not around,
Do you portray,
How you really think,
And not what you do?
This person you say is a friend,
But would they do it to you?

Stop! Wait a minute,
Would you want them to see,
What you're saying about them?
Is this how it should be?

If they walked through the door,
Would you turn right round?
Could you look them in the face,
Or would you look at the ground?
Where would you turn?
What could you say?
Nothing might change how they feel,
They could just walk away.

Is this how it should be?

It could all end up bad,
And you might just moan,
But you'll be the one,
All left on your own.
Do yourself a favour,
And sort out your life,
Cause all your gossiping,
Will only bring you strife.

Is this how it should be?

THROW IT ALL AWAY

You know in what you believe,
As you dance the night away;
A woman comes over to where you are,
And says 'Do you wanna go this way?'
Your heart starts to beat,
Faster than ever before;
She walks out of the room,
And through the open door.

Would you throw it all away,
In one moment of madness,
For something that will only,
Bring you times of sadness?

While you stand there thinking,
Another man walks over too;
'I want to show you something,
That might just interest you.'
He points towards his pocket and,
Your life is filled with fear;
He says 'Let's go outside,
I can't show you in here.'

You know what is wrong,
And you know full well what's right;
You walk out of another door,
And into the moonlit night.
Don't give in to all these lies,
Cause they won't make you fine;
You know you should be walking,
Along a different line.

Don't throw it all away,
For one moment of madness;
For something that will only,
Bring you times of sadness;
Don't throw it all away.

STEP OUT

You're walking along the road,
Following all the rules;
It's the only way forward,
But people say it's not cool.
You look out to the side,
And all that you can see;
You take another look forward,
It's all that you think you need.

If you step out of line,
Will you come back?
You may think you will,
But it's not as easy as that.

Can't believe what you are seeing,
People step out from the side;
Some in front of you,
Some way back behind.
Thinking for a minute,
Maybe I can do it too?
Some people probably can,
But is one of them you?

C

LEAVE IT ALL BEHIND

Leave it all behind,
You don't need it any more.

Life, oh how it changes,
And in so many ways;
Some things you were doing,
That you're not doing today.
Sometimes you wanna go back,
But soon you realise,
Your life's so much different now,
It's got no place in your eyes.

Leave it all behind,
What do you want it for?

There's so much more on offer,
Than you could ever think;
There's so much more to life,
Now you've found the missing link.
But sometimes you wonder why,
You've changed all your ways,
And then you'll know why you did it,
When you hear somebody say,

Leave it all behind,
You don't need it any more.
Leave it all behind,
What do you want it for?

BRIAN'S DREAM

Brian's dream was to see
The whole world saved;
He thought he could do it himself,
And that was the mistake he made.

He tried all he could,
To bring others to glory,
But his heart attitude was wrong,
And it was always the same old story.

People looked him in the face,
And could see right through,
And thought to themselves,
I don't wanna be like you.

Cause Brian's life was one big lie,
Although he may have been good;
He never lived his life,
In the way that he should.

He used to put himself first,
And Jesus last;
People just looked at him,
And walked right past.

If he thought for a minute,
And took one step back,
And gave it all to God,
He'd be back on the right track,

Cause God can't use you,
Unless you give it all;
If you put him first,
Then you'll hear the call.

END OF THE WORLD

Guns blazing. Shadows chasing;
The world's amazing.
What's going wrong? What's going on?
The world is going crazy.
Can you see it? Can you believe it?
Can you feel it?
It's going bad. Everybody's going mad.
This has surely got to end.

Is this,
The end of the world?
Is this,
The end of the world?

People crying. People dying.
People lying.
When will it stop? Who's at the top?
Is there anyone in charge?
Can you cope, when there's no hope?
Rocking the boat.
Chaos everywhere. They stand and stare.
No-one knows what to do.

Is this,
The end of the world?
Is this,
The end of the world?

HEART OF HEARTS

Down in your Heart of Hearts,
Do you know which way to go?
Down in your Heart of Hearts,
Are you sure?
Cause you know you want
So much more.

Just take a look at yourself,
Are you living as you should be?
When people take a look at you,
Who will they really see?
Will they see the real you,
Or the person you want them to see?
Open up your heart to God,
And he will set you free.

Give others the credit they deserve,
They're not as silly as you may think;
You're not going to fool anyone,
And you'll be the one to sink,
And disappear right out of sight,
Or slip to the back of the queue;
If you look into your heart right now,
It doesn't have to be you.

ICE RINK

We spend our time going round in circles,
Never getting anywhere.
Coming back to where we were before,
What did we achieve back there?
Some people pass on by,
But they're all on the same line.
How does it make you feel,
When you're looking at the wrong sign?

Round. Round. Round. Around we go,
Like we're on an Ice Rink.
Round. Round. Around we go.
Doesn't it make you think?
Round. Round. Round. Around we go,
We gotta change our style.
Round. Round. Around we go,
Cause we'll miss it by quite a mile.

We can never seem to stand up,
For what we believe;
People walk all over us,
If we could only see.
Trying so hard to get up,
But slipping back down again;
Reaching out to the side,
And then trying it again.

Round. Round. Round. Around we go,
Like we're on an Ice Rink.
Round. Round. Around we go.
Shouldn't it make us think?
Round. Round. Round. Around we go,
Are we gonna change our style?
Round. Round. Around we go.
Let's make that final mile.

We finally succeed in standing up,
To do what we know is right,
Only to be knocked down again;
We know we're in a fight.
We can only get it right,
We can begin to learn,
How to live our lives properly,
And make that important turn.

TIME

Go out and witness,
For our God the King;
Give yourself completely,
And he'll give you everything.
It won't be easy,
But you've got to have a go;
Some will say 'Yes',
Although others will say 'No'.

If you don't speak out,
You may regret it all,
When friends of yours, fall by your side,
Cause you disobeyed the call.
So spend a bit of time,
And spread the word of hope,
Cause if you don't do this,
Then you could be pulling their rope.

You don't have to be clever,
You may even think you're thick;
But it's what is deep down inside of you,
And what makes you really tick.
Anyone can witness,
It's really not so bad;
Just give yourself a chance,
You could be the only one they have.

Make the most,
Of the time you've got;
No matter what you think,
It really ain't a lot.
Time is gradually,
Running away.
Who's to say,
It won't end today?

WHAT IN THE WORLD!

It was created in only six days,
The seventh day he took a rest;
Two thousand years later on,
Is it still looking its best?
How can we lie and say it is,
When we just don't seem to care?
You can't even do a single thing,
If you just stand around and stare.
What in the world are we doing,
To this world of ours?
What in the world are we doing,
No more trees and flowers?
Many things have come and gone,
Many things are no more;
Look what we're doing here,
Does anyone know the score?
Can you just watch and see it go,
Stand around and let it happen?
We gotta change the way we live,
And change this familiar pattern.

THERE IS AN ANSWER

There is an answer,
And it's not too far away;
There is an answer,
And you can find it today.

When it all seems lost,
And there's nowhere left to turn;
When the game seems like it's over,
Yet there's so much more to learn.
When there's no way out,
That you can find to go;
When your mind's full of confusion,
And there appears no hope,

There is an answer,
And it's not too far away;
There is an answer,
And you can find it today.

If you wanna change your life,
And you don't know what to do;
If you wanna make a clean break,
And be a different you.
If you think that you can do it,
And believe that you really could;
If you wanna start a new life,
And make the change for good,

There is an answer,
And it's not too far away;
There is an answer,
And you can find it today.

LIVING ON THE EDGE

Living on the Edge. Living on the Edge.
We all wanna take, the
Easy way out; easy way out.
Living on the Edge.

Day by day, life goes by,
Changing all the time;
We have to make decisions,
Life is never the same.

We are undecided in what we should do,
Which way we should go.
Let's not make a decision at all,
Who is going to know?

Life ain't so simple,
Decisions we have to make;
It's all part of living,
We can't take a back seat,

Sometimes we have to say 'Yes',
Sometimes we say 'No'.
It's being able to know the difference,
Which one to go with.

Living on the Edge. Living on the Edge.
We all wanna take, the
Easy way out; easy way out.
Living on the Edge.

NO NEED FOR IT

I see you around quite a lot,
Sometimes you're just yourself,
But then I'll see you another day,
And I find it hard to tell,

That it's you,
The same person that I know.
Just who are you trying to fool?
You're only fooling yourself.

There's no need for it,
No. No need for it.

You don't have to impress anyone,
We will like you the same;
Probably even more in fact,
Stop playing your silly game,

Just be you,
The person we want to know;
Stop trying to fool everyone,
It's no good for yourself.

There's no need for it,
No. No need for it.

VOICES ALL AROUND ME

God cries out 'I love you son.
Come to me and I will forgive you.'
The devil calls out 'Lies. Lies.
I can give you far more.'
I don't know which way to turn.
Is it the devil or God calling me?
Voices are all that I can hear.

Christians call out 'Come to my Church,
We have the only answer.'
Your friends say 'Are you coming out?
Let's go to the Pub or the Disco.'
Turning one way, then the other,
The devil's way, God's way;
Oh won't somebody help me.

Voices all around me,
They circle inside my head,
Trying to make sense of what they say.
Mixed messages go round and round,
Who is telling the truth?

Jehovah's Witnesses they say they are right.
Why don't you join us?
My head says yes to all of them, but
My heart says no, except one that is;
That deep sinking feeling inside of me,
The love of God shining through.
Please God show yourself clearly to me.

The devil drifts off a defeated man,
'I'll be back to gain my revenge.'
The voices still go spinning around inside of me,
But there is only one voice,
That speaks clearly through to me,
And that is, the Lord and mighty God;
Jesus Christ, my mighty saviour.

I CAN HEAR HIM

There is someone up there,
Who has a plan for our lives,
And if we open up to him,
He will gradually reveal it to us.
If I listen to what he says,
He will show me where I went wrong;
He is always speaking out to me,
And if I listen, I can hear him.

I speak to him every day;
He is always there,
To help me when I need him,
Or to thank him for the things he does.
The Lord is a mighty God,
Who will always be there for me;
I need him in my life,
And if I listen, I can hear him.

Even before I gave my life to him,
He was there with me,
Listening to what I used to say,
Most of which he didn't like;
Then I heard him for the first time,
In a way I'd never done before;
He could hear me then, but now,
I can hear him as well.

I can hear him,
His voice ringing out;
Above all the other voices,
His voice rings out to you.
I can hear him, but can you?

THE DEVIL'S CHASING AFTER YOU

Carelessly walking the streets
In the dead of the night
On your own, there is no-one around;
What an awesome sight.
You hear footsteps behind you,
You quicken up your pace,
Not waiting to see who it is,
Running like you're in a race.

The devil's chasing after you.

Down the dark alleys you go,
Trying to find a place to hide;
But it is no use,
God knows where you are.
The devil he's not far behind,
You'd better watch out;
One little mistake
Could ruin it all.

The devil's chasing after you.
He won't stop until he's got you.

The devil will never let up,
Until he's got you on his side.
You turn around a corner,
There is no way out.
You look up, God is calling,
There's no need to run any more;
He is there, he will save you,
Give your life to him.

The devil's chasing after you.
He won't stop till he's got you;
Looking to destroy you;
You better watch out.

THERE'S NOTHING THAT I CAN DO

All over the world,
There is bitterness and suffering;
The arguments they still rage on,
Many people dying for their causes;
Tragedies striking the world.
But are they all necessary?
People turn to the Lord God,
Why don't you stop what's going on?

The Lord he looks in anguish,
People killing each other for no reason.
Why do they do it? Nobody knows.
Look at the mess the world is in,
Don't just stand and stare;
Surely there is something that you can do.
You're destroying the world, not God;
Something has got to be done.

Men walk round the streets,
Guns in their hands shooting at will;
People falling by the wayside.
Why, why do they do it?
Only they will know.
Is it really worth the bother?
What will it achieve,
If anything at all?

Most of the time it only causes
Heartbreak and suffering for too many people.
Why don't we just stop right now?
Most of the world would love that day.
But there are just those few,
Who don't really give a damn
As to what happens to this world,
As they destroy it more each day.

'There's nothing that I can do.
No. No. No. Nothing' the Lord cries out,
'You bring it all upon yourselves,
If only you stopped to think
What you're doing to my world.
I gave you all a free will,
And this is what you do;
There is nothing that I can do.'

GENERATIONS

Generations,
They come and go,
But still God is the same,
As when the first man walked,
And you walk today.

Years go by,
But still he's always there,
And will always be,
Loving you and everybody else;
He will never let you go.

Generation after generation
The Lord God is the same;
He's been here for thousands of years,
And he'll be there for evermore.

Lifetimes pass,
You think he's gone,
But he hasn't,
And he never will;
He is always there.

Another generation goes,
Is God still there?
You must surely know,
The answer by now;
He will never leave.

OCEAN BLUE

I sit alone and long to feel your love,
Flow right through me;
I know there's a God above,
Reaching out,
To where I know you are;
I long to feel your loving touch,
Come down upon my heart.

Your love flows through,
Like an Ocean Blue;
Your glorious love.
What more can I do,
To thank you for the things you've done?
I know you are the number one.

We turn away but still you are there,
You will never leave us,
Even when we don't care;
You look down,
To right where we are,
A sense of peace comes right through us
As you move upon our hearts.

FULL CONTROL

When you commit your life to him,
You're no longer the one in control;
You're handing the reins over to him.
Let him show you the way,
And the plan he has for you;
You've gotta let him have full control.

Full Control.
Have you let him take it?
Full Control.
That's what he wants.
Will you let him have it?
Full Control.

Things come up, which you wanna do,
Take time to think about it,
And what is best for you,
And what the Lord would want;
Let him make the decisions for you,
It's what the Lord would want;
Let him make the decisions for you,
Just let him take full control.

Full Control.
Have you let him take it?
Full Control.
That's what he wants.
Will you let him have it?
Full Control.

You gotta have someone,
Who is in control of your life;
Decisions, they could make or break you.
But if someone has control over them,
It would become much easier;
Go on give God, full control.

THE WATCHMAN

Every single minute of the day,
Looking down on your life,
There is someone,
Whether you know that or not;
He is with us, protecting us,
Forever he will be there.

He is the Watchman of our lives;
He made us his own, all those years ago.
He died on the cross, just to save our sins;
He forgives us when we do wrong, the Watchman is there.

Walking down the streets
You look over your shoulder,
No-one is there but you hear a voice;
'I am there with you, although you cannot see me,
I will never leave you or forsake you;
Forever I will be there,

'I am the Watchman of your life;
I made you my own, all those years ago.
I died on the cross, to save your sins;
I forgive you when you are wrong. I am the Watchman.'

You put a foot out of line;
You've made a mistake.
The Watchman he won't worry,
If you ask him for forgiveness.
'I Love you,' you call out to him.
'You are forgiven my son,' he replies.

You are the Watchman of my life;
You made me your own, all those years ago.
You died on the cross, to save my sins;
You forgive me when I do wrong. You are my Watchman.

KELSHONA BEACH

Your friends say are you going,
You don't know what to do;
You know you shouldn't really,
But everybody's going too.
If you don't go along with them,
What will they say?
Will they still be friends with you?
Your mind's in disarray.

Some have gone there once before,
And not come back again.
Will you make the same mistake,
And go along with them?
You must stand up for yourself,
And for what you believe;
They're not really friends of yours,
If they won't let you leave.

You watch from a distance,
As your friends go on down,
To Kelshona Beach;
You can't hear a sound,
You turn to walk away from there,
Cause you know you are right.
You shouldn't really be there;
The beach disappears from sight.

Kelshona Beach,
It's the place they all go,
It's not somewhere you'd wanna be,
If you were all alone.
Kelshona Beach,
People in the shadows.
Watch out what you do,
And who you get to know.

SOME THINGS ARE BEST FORGOTTEN

Some things are best forgotten,
Remember them no more;
We must carry on with life,
And firmly close the door.

Whenever we get a moment,
Our minds wander to the past,
Remembering the days so long ago;
Oh time it goes so fast.
Some times we're happy,
Some times we're sad;
Times of great enjoyment,
Times that made us mad.

Look towards the future,
And not back again;
Times that really hurt us,
There's no need to remember them.
The past will never help us.
What can we learn?
Many things have changed since then;
We've really got to turn.

All those things that happened then,
Nothing can change that now;
It's all gone forever,
But we don't know how.
One minute things are there,
The next they are gone;
Life is changing everyday;
We must stop holding on.

MATERIAL POSSESSIONS

At work you are the one,
The one they all talk about;
Driving around in your brand-new Porsche,
With girls sitting by your side.

When you're not in your car,
You can usually be found in a club,
Dancing the night away;
You never hear what they say.

You sit and stare at your beautiful house,
Five bedrooms it may have;
To you your luxuries mean a lot,
But when you are gone they mean nothing.

In your rooms, pictures adorn the wall,
Heroes of your day and the past;
You love them all, you love them all,
There's more to life than them.

Material Possessions are just for life,
What use are they when you're dead and gone?
They're no use where you are going,
Can't you see you are wrong?

HEARTFELT CRY

You talk to me and I listen,
To what you want to say;
You tell me about your feelings,
And how they won't go away,

And I listen,
Your heart crying out to me;
And I listen,
It's where you want me to be.

Sharing your thoughts and your troubles,
Sometimes I feel the same;
We can battle through it,
It all seems like a game,

And I listen,
Your heart crying out to me;
And I listen,
It's where you want me to be.

These things are sent to try us,
I know you know that too;
With his help you can do it,
But I'll be there for you,

And I listen,
Your heart crying out to me;
As I listen,
It's where I will always be.

E

DRIFT THROUGH THE TIMES

I used to talk to you,
But you never listened;
You were always in a different world,
Thinking about the past,
And the times you enjoyed before.

You walk through the streets,
The sound ringing in your ears,
But they do not register;
The times come flooding back,
The days you thought you enjoyed.

Drift through the times,
Your mind used to wander;
Drift through the times,
You were always in the past.

You don't have to live in the past,
Today is just as good,
But you haven't found that love.
You listen to your thoughts,
And the lies they're telling you.

There's only one way to enjoy yourself,
And he's been here all the time;
Past or present, he doesn't care,
He will always love you,
No matter what.

Drift through the times,
You don't have to any more;
Drift through the times,
The future is so clear.

NEXT TO YOU

When you rose up into Heaven,
From the mountain top,
Your life on Earth it ended,
But your love it never stopped.
You'll love me for ever,
No matter what I do;
One day I'll be in Heaven,
Sitting next to you.

ROAD TO DESTRUCTION

It's in our power to change the world,
Now that we have the love of God;
We can go around, and tell others about him,
And they will come to him.
Many people don't know they're wrong,
So it's up to us to tell them,
Or we'll be signing their death warrant,
Cause they'll keep on walking . . . . the Road to Destruction.

The Road to Destruction is the only way they know,
Knowing no different and what they have to live for;
No-one's ever told them about God,
And it's up to us to change that now!

We gave our lives to God for a reason,
Because we loved him and wanted to thank him
For dying on the cross for us;
So let's give someone else a chance,
To do the same thing.
We are not a selfish people,
Let's do something for him now;
The Road to Destruction is creeping closer.

The Road to Destruction is the only way they know,
Knowing no different and what they have to live for;
No-one's ever told them about God,
And it's up to us to change that now!

They're playing right into Satan's grasp,
Getting closer by the minute,
Yet they can't see it;
Closer and closer they go,
Towards the red-hot burning fire.
We've got to step in,
Before it's too late,
And show them the way they should go.

Many people are on the Road,
Some our Friends and Relatives.
Don't let the devil steal their lives.
Do something about it and quick,
Or they'll keep on heading down that road,
And then it will be too late.
There will be no turning back;
The Road to Destruction will have won.

WILL THERE BE A TOMORROW?

You've been to Church quite a few times,
First off it was just a joke,
But as the weeks went by,
You listened more intensely;
Many spoke to you about God,
And asked you if you were a Christian;
You tried to dodge the questions,
Without success most of the time.
'I'll do it next week,' you used to say.
'But will there be a next week?' came the reply.
'Will there be a tomorrow?'

Will there be a tomorrow?
You never know what will happen,
And what life has in store for you;
You could die tonight.

This thought stuck in your mind;
Surely they're only joking you used to say.
I'll be here next week and the week after that,
It won't be all over tonight, surely?
It won't be all over tonight.
I'll give my life to him when I'm dying;
Let me enjoy myself first.
'But what happens if you die suddenly?' they would say.
'You could be on your way to hell.
You've heard the phrase, here today, gone tomorrow.
Will there be a tomorrow?'

SEEING IS BELIEVING

Seeing is believing,
If you weren't already sure;
There's so much more to life,
Than you've ever thought before.
Open your eyes to everything there is,
Cause all that's before you,
He freely gives.

Seeing is believing,
If you'll only give it a go;
You won't know till you've tried it,
You realiy can't say 'No'.
There might be only one chance,
To see this for yourself;
If this doesn't convince you,
There isn't really much else.

LOVE LIKE THIS

I stand alone,
In the centre of this crowd;
I look around,
And want to shout out loud.
This feeling of love,
That's come upon me,
Is different to anything else;
What more can I need!

No love like this,
I've never felt like this before;
I really think I want some more,
Of this love.

Every single day,
I long to feel this love;
So all I do,
Is to say to the one above,
This feeling of love,
That you give to me,
It's better than anything else;
It's all that I need!

LIKE CHILDREN

Look around the room,
And what can you see?
The faces of these children,
As happy as can be,
Filled with the love of Jesus;
They can teach us a thing.
Let's open our eyes,
And acknowledge him as king.
A childlike faith is what we need,
Let's read the Bible and begin to feed,
On the word of God and what he can give;
Let's come like children and begin to live,
Innocent and Honest,
That's how we should be;
Not worried who's around us,
And who is watching me;
Give all our problems to him,
Don't worry about a thing.
Let's come before him,
And acknowledge him as king.

BEAT THE CLOCK

You try to beat the clock
Before you finally knock,
On the door to eternal life.
If you leave it too long,
You might hear the bong,
And then it will be too late.

If you ask, it shall be given,
Unto you;
Seek and you will find.
Knock on the door, and
It shall be opened;
You don't wanna be left behind.

You could run it close,
But then again who knows?
When your time is up,
When your number's called,
You don't wanna be fooled,
Cause you don't really know.

YOU'LL BE SORRY

You'll be sorry you left when you did,
Left the argument unfinished;
It's best not to go to sleep,
Until your mind is at rest.

What if something happened,
And you still weren't right with them,
Would you be able to live with yourself,
Without making your peace?
What's the point in arguing?
What does it resolve?
People finish up getting hurt,
And no-one wins in the end.

All it needs is a bit of sense,
Even meet them halfway;
Someone to compromise their position,
Or someone to make a stand.
The sun may go down on the day,
But the problems don't stop there;
People remember arguments,
And can bring them up again.

ONE-WAY TICKET

I walked into the station foyer,
A quiet deserted place,
Except for an old man reading a paper,
But I couldn't see his face.

I moved over towards the ticket office,
And the attendant looked up at me,
'What do you want?' he said.
'I want a one-way ticket please.'

A One-Way Ticket to Heaven,
There's nowhere I'd rather go.
A One-Way Ticket to Heaven,
Can I have something to show?

The attendant punched in some buttons,
And the machine made a funny sound;
The ticket appeared in front of him;
It was a funny sort of brown.

I went to go for my wallet,
But he said 'You don't need money.'
As he handed over the ticket,
He said to me 'Enjoy your journey.'

I went through the swinging doors,
To walk towards the train;
The old man still sitting there;
I walked out into the rain.

I strolled along the platform,
Where many had gone before;
There were some people waiting,
And there would be many more.

Then a sound came from the distance,
At first it didn't seem loud,
But the nearer and nearer it came,
The more people joined the crowd.

The train gradually came to a halt,
And the people looked on in awe,
Our tickets at the ready
As we waited to climb aboard.

As I sat in the corner of the train,
I thought about the old man I'd seen;
I looked out of the window
To where he once had been.

The train slowly moved away
And off through the driving rain,
And then the old man reappeared,
But unfortunately he'd missed the train.